Bunny-wool Blockade

by Paul Stewart
Illustrated by Bill Ledger

OXFORD
UNIVERSITY PRESS

In this story ...

Cam
(Switch)

Cam has the power to turn into different animals. She once stopped some baddies from robbing a bank by turning into a giraffe.

Nisha
(Nimbus)

Evan
(Flex)

Slink
(Combat Cat)

Chapter 1:
Carrots for breakfast

Cam stared down at the bowl in front of her. "Carrot soup for breakfast?" she said.

Nisha wrinkled her nose at the carrot muffin on her plate. Along the table she saw Evan pulling a face, and all around them other pupils were grumbling. Even Slink looked unhappy.

"I'm sorry," said Miss Baker, who was pushing
a trolley while Mrs Butterworth served soup.
"The delivery man didn't come this morning.
I don't know why."

"So we had to make do," added Mrs Butterworth.
"All we had left was a bag of carrots."

Cam tried a spoonful of the carrot soup. Nisha
nibbled her carrot muffin.

"I prefer cornflakes," said Cam.

After breakfast, the two girls went into the kitchen to see if there was anything they could do to help. They found Mrs Butterworth and Miss Baker staring at the empty shelves.

"What are we going to do for lunch?" Miss Baker said with a sigh.

"We could go into the city and get some supplies," Cam suggested.

"That would be helpful," said Mrs Butterworth. "I've already written a list."

Mrs Butterworth handed Cam and Nisha the list, and the girls set off. They didn't get very far.

"The back door won't open," said Cam.

"That's odd," said Miss Baker. "Are you sure?"

Cam tried the door again. "It won't budge." She crouched down, looked through the cat-flap … and saw a pair of white trousers and two shiny black shoes.

Chapter 2:
Under siege

"Bunny-wunnies," came a harsh voice, "bring me something to kneel on. I don't want to get my suit dirty."

Cam saw a mat drop to the ground, then a pair of knees. She leaned forward for a closer look and gave a startled cry as two eyes stared back at her.

"Oh no!" Cam said.

"Who is it?" asked Nisha.

"Ray Ranter, that's who!" came the answer through the cat-flap.

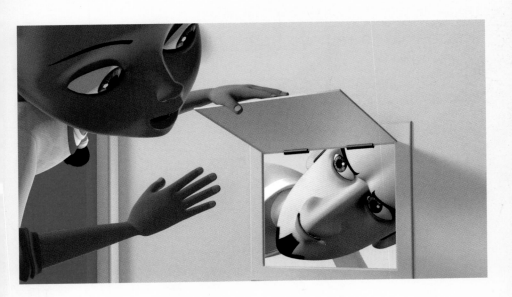

Ray Ranter

Catchphrase: Heroes are zeroes!

Hobbies: stamp collecting. He would love nothing more than to have a set of Ranter stamps.

Likes: white rooms, white suits, turnips (because they're white).

Dislikes: all colours, and raspberries (because they're hairy, and raspberry stains are impossible to remove from white suits).

Beware! He created robotic rabbits – bunny-wunnies – to help him carry out his dastardly plans.

Cam groaned. Ray Ranter was the arch-enemy of Hero Academy.

Just then, Evan ran in. "The front door is blocked!" he gasped.

"You're trapped!" Ranter told them gleefully. "All the doors to the school have been barricaded with planks of wood."

"Why?" asked Cam.

Ranter didn't answer – he just pushed a piece of paper through the cat-flap.

"What's this?" Cam asked, taking the piece of paper.

"An important document that says I'm the new owner of Hero Academy," Ranter told her. "You must get it signed. Then the school will belong to me."

"WHAT?" Cam yelled. "No way!"

"I'm afraid you have no choice. You see, I'm going to turn the building into a museum when you lot have gone," he said. "A very special museum. The Ray Ranter Museum. A museum all about *me*." He grinned nastily.

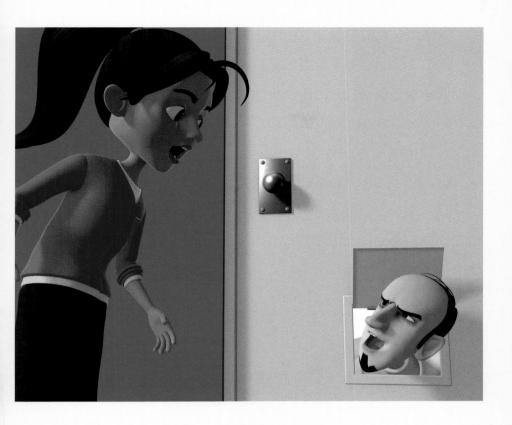

"There will be photographs, films, newspaper clippings and holograms about my wonderful life and successful career," Ranter continued. "There will also be a special room about how I finally managed to close down Hero Academy." Then he began to laugh. "Mwah-ha-ha-ha!"

Nisha peered at Ranter through the cat-flap. "If you want to get us out, why have you locked us in?" she asked.

"I know you superheroes. You'll refuse to go,"
Ranter answered with a sneer, "but without any
supplies, you'll soon be desperate to leave." His
eyes narrowed. "Hang on," he said. "There's one
more thing I need to do."

Ranter disappeared. Cam and Nisha saw lots
of bunny-wunnies through the cat-flap. Some of
them were surrounding the delivery van and a very
confused-looking driver.

Cam turned to Nisha and Evan. "This is awful," she said. "Hero Academy is in real danger."

"Either we get that document signed," said Nisha, "or we go hungry." She shuddered. "If only Pip was here. She could break the door down."

Unfortunately, Pip was with a group of pupils that Mr Trainer and Miss Linen had taken to Shivertop Mountain, north of Lexis City. They were practising their superhero skills in the snowy conditions.

Cam, Nisha and Evan were due to go the following week, but that would only happen if they could save the school.

Ranter reappeared at the cat-flap. "I've turned off the water supply," he said. "Now, you've got nothing to drink either."

"Don't think your friends will come to rescue you any time soon," he added. "My blizzard machine has seen to that."

Cam gasped. "I hope they're all right."

Chapter 3:
Time to save Hero Academy

From outside, there came the sound of Ranter's horrible laughter. "Mwah-ha-ha-ha!"

"Come on," said Cam. "It's up to us to save Hero Academy." She crumpled Ranter's piece of paper. "We need to get out of here and defeat Ray Ranter and his army of bunny-wunnies. Let's fetch the others. We'll go up to the roof and see what we can do."

From the top of the building, it was clear that the whole school was surrounded.

Slink was the first to try to escape. As Combat Cat, he slid down the roof, scrambled down the wall and used his karate skills to beat a path through the bunny-wunnies. The trouble was, there were just too many of them. Together, they chased after Combat Cat, and he had to climb a drainpipe to get away.

Evan tried next. He used his super-stretchy legs to climb down from the roof. However, the bunny-wunnies soon spotted him. They pulled off his shoes and tickled his feet. Evan had to give up because he couldn't stop laughing.

"Let me have a go," said Nisha. She made torrential rain pour down from a huge black cloud overhead ... but the bunny-wunnies had come prepared.

"Give up!" shouted Ranter, raising his umbrella in the air.

"Well, I for one will *never* give up," Cam told the others. "I've got an idea. Those carrot muffins will come in useful after all. If you lot distract the bunny-wunnies with them, I'll make my escape."

Chapter 4:
Trapped

Cam, Nisha and Evan went back to the kitchen. Mrs Butterworth and Miss Baker gave them the uneaten muffins, then Nisha and Evan returned to the roof. Meanwhile, Cam turned into Switch, looked out of the cat-flap and waited.

Soon, it was raining carrot muffins as Nisha, Evan and the others threw them off the roof. The bunny-wunnies went crazy as they fought each other for the delicious carrot snacks.

"That should keep them busy," Switch said.

It was time for her to act. She changed into a mouse. Then, when the bunny-wunnies weren't looking, she scampered through the cat-flap.

Switch's whiskers twitched as she looked around. Things were worse than she'd feared. The door was nailed firmly shut, and there seemed to be even more of Ranter's one-eyed bunny-wunnies than before. They were everywhere!

Ranter himself was standing with a megaphone in his hand.

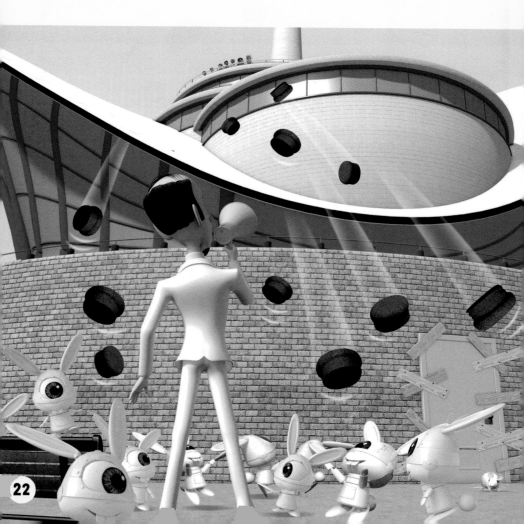

"You won't stop me that easily!" Ranter bellowed. "Are you getting hungry and thirsty yet? Those carrot muffins have all gone now, and the bunny-wunnies are ready to attack. You cannot win. Sign the document. Give yourselves up and ..." Then he saw the mouse. "Aaaaaargh!" he screamed and jumped up on to a bench.

"Clever Switch," said Nisha. "She must have known Ranter was afraid of mice." Then she called down, "Go away!"

"Never!" Ranter shouted back. "Bunny-wunnies, catch that mouse and bring it to me."

His army of robotic bunnies immediately went hopping after Switch. They opened the hatches in their tummies and each pulled out a net.

"Uh oh!" Switch thought, as she scurried away. Zigzagging left and right, she dodged the bunny-wunnies' nets, but then disaster struck.

THWAP! A net came down over her.

"Trapped!" said Ranter. He took the net from the bunny-wunny and held it in the air. "Mwah-ha-ha-ha!"

Chapter 5:
Rhino rescue

Switch looked around miserably. "*Now* what?" she thought. She was just about to turn herself back to normal when a much better idea occurred to her. Concentrating hard, she transformed into … a rhinoceros!

The huge animal burst out of the net. Ranter stumbled back and fell to the ground.

The bunny-wunnies blocked the way between the rhino and the back door of Hero Academy. With an angry grunt, Switch lowered her head and charged. The bunny-wunnies scattered, squeaking loudly as they hopped out of her way. Switch ran faster and faster.

BANG! She crashed into the door. The wood splintered. The planks were smashed to pieces. The door was broken down.

Mrs Butterworth, Miss Baker, Nisha, Evan and all the others came pouring out. The bunny-wunnies put their paws up and surrendered.

Suddenly, Ranter's helicopter appeared in the sky. A bunny-wunny sat at the controls. It lowered a rope for Ranter.

Ranter sprinted towards the rope, jumped up and grabbed it. The army of bunny-wunnies hopped after the helicopter. They leaped up and tried to cling on anywhere they could.

"I'll get you next time!" Ranter's voice floated back, as the helicopter flew away.

Everyone ignored him. They were looking at Switch, who had changed back into Cam. She straightened her top and smiled.

"Another job well done," she said, dusting herself down.

The others whooped and cheered. Then they all marched back into the academy, along with the delivery man, who was finally able to give them their supplies.

"We'll make the best lunch Hero Academy has ever seen," said Mrs Butterworth happily.

"We certainly shall," said Miss Baker.

Just then, the school bus returned from Shivertop Mountain. Ben, Pip, Jin and Axel explained how they'd dug their way out of the snowed-in cabin. Then Cam told them everything that had happened while they'd been away.

"He wanted to turn the academy into the Ray Ranter Museum," Cam explained.

"He failed," Nisha added. "Thanks to Cam."

"Ray Ranter may like bunny-wunnies," Cam said, giggling, "but he's terrified of mice!"